The College Softball Recruiting Process

How to get recruited.

Howard E. Deihl, RHU

Published by Howard E. Deihl, RHU

4400 State Hwy 121, Suite 300
Lewisville, TX 75056
www.thegeneralagency.com

Deihl, Howard E., RHU

Title: The Softball Recruiting Process
          How to get recruited

ISBN: 979-8-8690-2704-7

Imprint: Independently published

Printed in the United States of America

Cover design by Howard E. Deihl, RHU

10 9 8 7 6 5 4 3 2 1

Table of Contents

Chapter One   1
Introduction   1

Chapter Two   4
Softball Scholarships and Recruitment   4
    The NCAA   4
    The NAIA   6
    The NJCAA   7
    The CCCAA   8
    Softball Scholarships Break Down   9
    NCAA Scholarship Distribution   9
    NAIA scholarship Distribution   10
    NJCAA or Junior College   10
    Recruiting Timeline by High School Grade 11
    College Coaches Communication   11
    High Schools Timelines   12
    Social Media Recruitment   12

Chapter Three   14
Softball Recruiting is Like Dating   14

Chapter Four

College Tuition

Chapter Four   18

College Tuition   18

What is College Tuition?   18

Is it worth it?   19

In-State and Out-of-State Tuition   20

In-State Tuition   20

Out-of-State Tuition   21

Challenges of Out-of-State Tuition   21

Weighing the Options   22

Chapter Five   24

Securing a Softball Scholarship   24

Athletic Skill   24

Academic Performance   26

Strategic Outreach   27

Chapter Six   30

The Softball Players Responsibilities   30

Social Media Dos and Don'ts   34

General Tips For Softball Players   37

Chapter Seven   44

Comprehensive Training and Teaching Scenarios   44

The Softball Coach's Responsibilities   44

Prioritizing All Players Over Wins   45

Leveraging Losses as Teaching Opportunities   45

Supporting Struggling Players   46

Creation of Player Profiles   46

Communicating with College Coaches   47

Chapter EIGHT   49

Parents' Responsibilities   49

Positive Behavior at Games   49

Be On Time for Games and Practices   50

Uniform Maintenance   50

Support Your Player's Practice Schedule   51

Provide Constructive Feedback   52

Chapter nine   56

Softball Skills Videos   56

Start with your introduction   56

Batting Skills   57

Base Running, sliding, and diving.   58

Videos by position   59

Pitchers   59

Catchers   60

Middle infielders   61

First Base   63

Third Base   64

Outfielders   65

Editing   66

Common Video Mistakes   66

Chapter ten   68

Unconventional Drills   68

Racquetball Court Drill for Softball Players   68

Hitting off an automated Pitching Machine   69

The Bat Throw Drill   70

Chapter Eleven   72

Softball Player's College Recruiting Checklist   72

About The Author   81

CHAPTER ONE

INTRODUCTION

As a seasoned softball coach with over two decades of experience, including eight successful years owning and operating Homerun Alley in Carrollton, Texas, I have had the privilege of seeing and helping hundreds of athletes achieve their dreams of playing college softball. This book, "Softball Recruiting," is a culmination of this experience, designed to guide aspiring softball players through the recruiting process and towards securing a college scholarship.

In "Softball Recruiting," I share my experience as a coach and mentor, having helped countless players find their way through the complexities of college recruitment. The thrill of watching these athletes' step onto a college field, with their expressions a blend of pride and excitement, is priceless. This book is my way of extending this mentor ship further, offering guidance to those aspiring to play college softball.

Whether you are driven by a passion for the game or a dream to play at the collegiate level, rest assured, there's a college out there for you. The key lies in identifying the right college and understanding the scholarship process.

In this book, you will find:

- Strategies for showcasing your skills, including the use of social media, email communication, creating impactful skills videos, and participating in camps and clinics.

- Comparisons between collegiate affiliations like NCAA and NAIA.

- Insights into scholarship distribution.

- The unique roles and duties of players, coaches, and parents in the recruitment process.

- Specialized tips for coaches to aid in player recruitment.

- The crucial role of parents in supporting and guiding their athlete.

- Detailed advice on player responsibilities to maximize scholarship chances.

- The significance of academic performance, stressing the importance of a high GPA and strong standardized test scores, such as the ACT and SAT.

Getting a softball scholarship is as much about personal development as it is about athletic ability. This book is intended to be a comprehensive guide, simplifying the recruitment process, and highlighting the importance of every step - from each swing and pitch to every academic achievement. Turn your softball dreams into reality. Good luck on your journey!

CHAPTER TWO

SOFTBALL SCHOLARSHIPS AND RECRUITMENT

In the United States, college softball teams span across various divisions and associations, each with its own unique characteristics and offerings. Understanding these divisions and offerings can help you decide on your athletic career opportunities.

THE NCAA

The NCAA (National Collegiate Athletic Association) has three major divisions:

- **Division I:** This division include approximately 300 teams. Division I schools are typically larger universities with more resources dedicated to their athletic programs. In terms of softball, Division I schools tend to have a more rigorous playing and training schedule, often competing against other high-level programs. Athletes in Division I can expect a strong commitment to their sport, with more scholarships available compared to the other divisions.

- **Division II:** This division encompasses approximately 300 teams. Division II schools are somewhat smaller, and the athletic programs are a bit less intense compared to Division I schools. Softball players still experience a competitive environment, but with a bit more balance between athletics and academics. Scholarships are offered, but they are fewer in comparison to Division I schools.

- **Division III:** Has approximately 400 teams. Division III prioritizes a balance between sports, academics, and extracurriculars. For softball, this means less focus on athletic scholarships and a more relaxed competition schedule. This division is a good fit for those who want to play softball in college but also want to explore other interests.

THE NAIA

The National Association of Intercollegiate Athletics (NAIA) plays a pivotal role in the world of collegiate sports, including softball, in the United States. It comprises around 200 teams, emphasizing a balanced approach to academics and athletics. This balance is particularly notable in the NAIA, as it frequently operates within smaller campus settings.

In these environments, students are often able to engage more deeply with both their academic and athletic commitments, benefiting from a more intimate campus experience. The smaller scale of NAIA institutions typically allows for closer interactions between students, faculty, and coaches, fostering a community-oriented atmosphere that can be highly appealing to many students.

This structure of the NAIA, with its focus on both educational and athletic growth, offers a unique and supportive environment for student-athletes. It caters to those who seek to excel in their sport while also prioritizing their academic journey, providing an ideal setting for personal and professional development.

THE NJCAA

The National Junior College Athletic Association (NJCAA) holds a vital place in collegiate softball in the United States, especially for community college athletes. In the NJCAA, colleges are divided into three divisions: Division I, II, and III. This division ensures schools with different resources and aims can compete fairly. With about 500 teams in these divisions, the NJCAA offers a wide range of opportunities for softball players, indicating robust participation and competitive levels.

One of the key features of the NJCAA is the provision of athletic scholarships in Divisions I and II. These scholarships are crucial for athletes seeking financial support to continue their education while playing softball. The NJCAA serves as an important platform for players to develop their skills and gain valuable competitive experience. For many, it acts as a gateway to further opportunities, such as transferring to four-year colleges or pursuing professional careers in softball.

Moreover, NJCAA programs, being part of community colleges, often provide a more balanced approach between academic pursuits and athletics. This balance is appealing to students who aim to excel in both their educational and athletic endeavors.

THE CCCAA

The California Community College Athletic Association (CCCAA) stands as a significant entity in the collegiate sports landscape, specifically in California. It incorporates around 100 teams, demonstrating a strong presence in the region's athletic scene.

The CCCAA's focus within California offers a unique platform for athletes, particularly those who are part of community colleges. This regional emphasis allows for a concentrated development of sports programs tailored to the needs and characteristics of California's diverse student population.

By hosting a substantial number of teams, the CCCAA creates an environment rich in competition and opportunities for athletes. This setting not only fosters athletic growth but also contributes to the broader educational experience of the students involved. The association's role in nurturing talent and providing competitive platforms in California is a key component of the state's community college system, enhancing the overall collegiate sports experience for many student-athletes.

SOFTBALL SCHOLARSHIPS BREAK DOWN

- **Full-ride Scholarship:** Most full-ride scholarships are given crucial positions such as pitchers and catchers. However other crucial positions can also provide full ride offers. Full rides generally cover all significant college expenses such as tuition, room, and board, and occasionally, even books are included.

- **Partial Scholarship:** This scholarship covers part of the tuition or other related expenses.

- **Walk-on:** This option is the doorway for players to step into the team without an immediate scholarship, with the potential to earn scholarships based on performance and contribution.

NCAA SCHOLARSHIP DISTRIBUTION

Each division has a limited number of scholarships based on the size of the college. Here is a breakdown by division:

- Division I: Each team has up to 12 full scholarships.

- Division II: A maximum of 7.2 full scholarships are allocated per team.

- Division III: This division prioritizes academics. Therefore, it does not offer athletic scholarships, but there are academic scholarships and other financial aid available.

NAIA SCHOLARSHIP DISTRIBUTION

NAIA has up to 10 scholarships for each team.

NJCAA OR JUNIOR COLLEGE

Offers 12 to 24 full scholarships depending on school size.

RECRUITING TIMELINE BY HIGH SCHOOL GRADE

The softball recruiting timeline by high school grade is a structured pathway that guides athletes through the process of being noticed, evaluated, and recruited by college coaches. Throughout this timeline, maintaining strong academic performance and actively participating in showcases or camps is essential for maximizing recruitment opportunities.

COLLEGE COACHES COMMUNICATION

- **Division I:** Coaches cannot communicate with players until September 1st of the players junior year of high school. However, player is encouraged to email these coaches as they will be clamoring for players on September 1st.

- **Division II, Division III, and NAIA:** coaches can communicate with the players select coach prior to the September 1st of the players junior year.

HIGH SCHOOLS TIMELINES

- **Freshman & Sophomore Years:** This is the beginning of competitive play, attending camps. It is important to start a portfolio with statistics and notable achievements.

- **Sophomore & Junior Years:** Promote your skills by creating videos that displays your abilities, accompanied by emailing college coaches and assistant coaches.

- **Junior Year:** Visit college campuses and if possible, engage with coaching staff, player and attend live games.

- **Senior Year:** Go on official visits when invited and have in-depth discussions concerning scholarships and defining your potential role in the team.

SOCIAL MEDIA RECRUITMENT

In this digital age, social media emerges as a powerful tool in the recruitment process. Take advantage of this by maintaining a positive on-line presence.

Having a personal website and dedicated social media accounts can be beneficial. On these platforms you can share all aspects of your softball experience, such as the hard work you put in during practice and the best plays from your tournaments. This will make it easy for college coaches to see your skills, dedication, and progress.

With this understanding of the college softball landscape, scholarships, and recruitment process, you can now begin to start the process.

CHAPTER THREE

SOFTBALL RECRUITING IS LIKE DATING

In my recruiting classes, I often draw on this analogy, mainly for its entertainment value. It never fails to draw laughter from players and parents, making it a memorable part of the speech. To clarify, I am not promoting dating among young people, and in the context of this chapter, the analogy is not gender neutral. It is not my intention to offend anyone, but I believe parents and coaches will grasp the sentiment.

I commonly use the following scenario: imagine you are at a high school dance, and you are captivated by a boy on the opposite side of the room. You may want to approach him and ask him to dance, but there is uncertainty – does he already have a girlfriend? He might also be glancing your way, hoping to dance with you, but is held back by the same doubt about whether you have a boyfriend. The only solution is to ask.

By the same token, college coaches are not magically aware of your desire to play for their team. They might spot you on the field, be impressed by your athleticism, but they remain in the dark about various details: Does my college offer the degree program the player is wanting? Do you want to remain in-state or venture out of state? Are you interested in another college?

Though, this is not directly comparable to the dance floor dynamic, at the field, neither you nor your parents should approach the coaches directly. This is the responsibility of your select coach.

Your part involves emailing the coaches from colleges you are interested in playing for. Email remains a reliable means to express your interest in their institution. Depending on your age and the NCAA rules governing the college, the coaches may not be able to reply to you directly. Yet, they can and often do, come to see you in action.

There are times, especially during camps and clinics, when face-to-face interactions with college coaches are possible. As trivial as it may sound, improving your communication skills for such encounters is crucial. Projecting confidence in your speaking skills can greatly influence a college coaches' ability to communicate with you.

When you participate in showcase tournaments, it is good practice to identify which colleges will be in attendance and whether or not they offer your desired degree program. In such instances, notify the prospective coaches about your games, ensuring to include field details and game times.

For select coaches attending showcase tournaments, it is important to have a profile sheet of all players displayed on the fence behind home plate. Assign a parent to keep an eye out for college coaches. If a college coach approaches your field, feel free to introduce yourself. Once introductions are out of the way, ask about the specific positions they are looking for, whether infield, outfield, hitters, or slappers. Clarify the graduation year they are considering. Your players should have informed you about the coaches they have contacted and who they invited to the game. It is essential to give priority to the player who "brought the coach to the dance".

It is important to remember that, whether attending a showcase tournament or not, players, parents, friends, and family should always behave as though they are being observed. In some cases, a college coach may not be able to attend, but they might send someone to observe the player. This representative will then report back to the coach on the player's performance and demeanor. I will cover more on this topic later in this book.

CHAPTER FOUR

COLLEGE TUITION

WHAT IS COLLEGE TUITION?

At its core, college tuition is the price one pays for instruction and learning at a college or university. It is the fundamental cost that is associated with gaining access to academic teachings, resources, and the institutional environment. Tuition may be charged on a per-credit basis, per course, or as a flat fee covering a full academic term or year.

Beyond tuition, there are additional costs that students commonly encounter, such as room and board, textbooks, supplies, and transportation. These additional costs, while not strictly tuition, significantly influence the total cost of attending college.

Scholarships, grants, and financial aid can offset tuition costs. Understanding these options is important when considering playing at the next level.

IS IT WORTH IT?

The short answer is yes! Although most college athletes graduate with some student loan debt, in most cases, it is substantially less than non-athletes. In addition to having lower student loan debt, most college athletes end up earning more throughout their working careers than non-athletes.

Consider this scenario: on average, as of 2022, a college graduate has a debt of $37,650, applicable to both athletes and non-athletes. This number may seem substantial; however, when you consider that it is less than the cost of a new car—which would only last about five years—a college education will last a lifetime. Additionally, college graduates generally earn considerably more over the course of their lifetimes compared to non-college graduates.

IN-STATE AND OUT-OF-STATE TUITION

One of the most significant considerations when considering a college or university revolves around in-state and out-of-state tuition.

IN-STATE TUITION

In-state tuition is a privileged rate given to students attending a public university or college within the state where they have established residency. This form of tuition is substantially reduced and is designed to promote education within one's home state, and to make higher education affordable to residents.

Benefits of In-State Tuition

- **Cost-Efficiency:** In-state tuitions are comparatively lower, easing the financial burden and helping access to education.

- **Local Opportunities:** Being close to home can cultivate connections, internships, and job opportunities within the state, leveraging local networks and resources.

- **Community Connection:** Attending a school within one's state can nurture a sense of community and belonging, creating a conducive environment for personal and academic growth.

OUT-OF-STATE TUITION

Out-of-state tuition applies to students who opt to attend a public university or college outside their state of residency. This form of tuition is typically higher, reflecting the institution's commitment to prioritize and subsidize education for its own state residents.

CHALLENGES OF OUT-OF-STATE TUITION

- **Financial Load:** The higher cost of out-of-state tuition can pose substantial financial challenges, often requiring careful planning and substantial investment.

- **Adaptability:** Venturing beyond state borders can require adaptability to new environments, cultures, and networks, requiring a strong support system and strength.

- **Competitive Admission:** The admission processes for out-of-state students can often be more competitive, requiring exceptional academic and extracurricular accomplishments.

WEIGHING THE OPTIONS

Understanding the comparative dynamics of in-state and out-of-state tuition is instrumental in making informed educational decisions.

- **Financial Aid and Scholarships:** While in-state tuition is essentially more affordable, out-of-state students may access various scholarships and financial aid opportunities that can substantially offset costs.

- **Return on Investment:** Paying out-of-state tuition might be justified through unique educational opportunities, networks, or career prospects that align with the student's aspirations.

- **Strategic Considerations:** Strategic considerations such as academic specializations, institutional reputation, and long-term career goals should be carefully weighed against the financial implications of tuition categories.

Each choice carries its own unique array of opportunities and challenges. With this understanding, students can improve their educational journey, that resonates with their aspirations, capabilities, and vision for the future.

CHAPTER FIVE

SECURING A SOFTBALL SCHOLARSHIP

Earning a softball scholarship requires a blend of both athletic and academic commitment. It is important to understand how to reach out to the right coaches and stand out amongst your competition. This chapter will explain three pivotal aspects you should focus on: Athletic Skill, Academic Performance, and Strategic Outreach.

ATHLETIC SKILL

- **Consistent Training:** While natural talent is beneficial, consistent training will always be the primary factor of skill development. It is crucial to train not only during the season but in the off-season as well. This might involve attending specialized softball camps, joining a select team, and/or personal coaching.

- **Specialization vs. Versatility:** While some coaches look for players with specialized skills, others value players who can perform well in multiple positions. Understand your strengths but also focus on developing versatility on the field.

- **Physical Fitness:** Softball demands agility, strength, and stamina. Regular conditioning, including cardiovascular workouts, strength training, and agility drills, can significantly enhance your performance.

- **Mental Strength:** Softball is as much a mental game as it is a physical one. Developing a strong mindset, understanding game strategy, and cultivating the ability to make quick decisions under pressure can set you apart.

ACADEMIC PERFORMANCE

- **The Balancing Act:** Remember, the term is "student-athlete." Many colleges prioritize athletes who also excel academically. Maintaining a high GPA can open more doors and make you a more appealing candidate.

- **NCAA Academic Eligibility:** To be recruited by NCAA schools, you must meet specific academic criteria. Familiarize yourself with these requirements early in your high school career to ensure you are on the right track.

- **Showcase Your Commitment:** Involvement in extra-curricular activities, honor societies, or community service demonstrates that you are well-rounded and can handle commitments both on and off the field.

- **Test Scores Matter:** For many institutions, standardized test scores still play a crucial role in admissions. Consider preparing for exams like the SAT or ACT with the same enthusiasm you would a big game.

STRATEGIC OUTREACH

- **Research:** Begin by listing colleges or universities that align with your academic and athletic aspirations. Research their softball programs, the coaching staff, and their style of play to see where you might fit in.

- **Initiate Contact:** Most coaches appreciate proactive athletes. Send them an introduction email with a link to your skills video or channel, your academic accomplishments, and a brief note on why you are interested in their program.

- **Attend Camps:** These events are designed for coaches to search for potential recruits. They offer you an opportunity to demonstrate your skills and directly interact with college coaches.

- **Attend Showcase Tournaments:** Showcase tournaments can be a bit tricky. In some instances, coaches may not be able to speak to you directly during a showcase, but they can communicate with your select coach. Although attending showcase tournaments is popular, there are essential steps to take beforehand.

First and foremost, you need to reach out to the college coach you want to play for. Send them your schedule, and express your interest in playing for their team, ensuring they can come to watch you. Merely attending a showcase does not guarantee that you will be noticed. You might be on the field all day without fielding a ball. Even if you are the best player on the field, not having opportunities to display your skills could leave you unnoticed.

Batting, on the other hand, is crucial during showcase tournaments. Coaches look for a perfect swing, regardless of whether contact is made. College coaches can help improve your ability to see the ball, but correcting bad mechanics is more challenging and time-consuming. Ensure your swing is flawless every time.

- **Follow-Up:** If a coach expresses interest, ensure you maintain regular communication. Update them on any new accomplishments or changes in your schedule. This not only shows your dedication but keeps you fresh in their minds.

- **Be Genuine:** Build genuine relationships with potential coaches. They are not just looking for great athletes, but individuals who will fit into their team culture and represent their institution positively.

While the path to securing a softball scholarship can be challenging, it is by no means unattainable. With a focused approach on enhancing your athletic skill, maintaining academic excellence, and strategic outreach, you will be well on your way to turning your college softball dreams into a reality.

CHAPTER SIX

THE SOFTBALL PLAYERS RESPONSIBILITIES

Securing a softball scholarship is not just a matter of luck or pure talent; it is a goal that requires commitment, strategic planning, and continuous effort from the player. It requires honing one's skills, building a strong athletic profile, and showcasing dedication and discipline both on and off the field. Players must not only become masters of the game, mastering the techniques and strategies required for exceptional performance, but also express dedication and a hunger for improvement.

Additionally, building a network, researching potential schools, and understanding the nuances of eligibility and the recruitment processes are essential steps to earning a scholarship. In this chapter we will dive into how you, as a player, can actively and effectively secure the softball scholarship.

1. **Commit to Rigorous Training:** Simply rolling off the couch and expecting to play college softball is not an option. To earn a softball scholarship, players must commit to a demanding and consistent training routine. This commitment is not solely about showing up for practice. It is about dedicating themselves to the mastery of the sport. Players are expected to constantly refine their skills, enhance their strategies, and strengthen both their physical fitness and mental toughness. Training is not confined to the softball field; it also includes personal fitness sessions, studying the game, and maintaining a healthy, athlete-oriented lifestyle.

2. **Setting Career Goals and Selecting a Major:** These are among the most important aspects to consider when aiming to play college softball. It is essential to ensure that the colleges you are considering offer your desired degree program. Choosing your career path early has its

advantages. Planning for your future post-graduation is significant. Remember, some students change majors while in college.

3. **Researching Potential Colleges:** When researching potential colleges. You may want to consider a few factors such as:

- **Degree Program:** Ensure that the college you are considering offers the degree program you want to pursue.

- **Location (In-State vs. Out-of-State):** In-state tuition rates are generally substantially less than out-of-state tuition. Some states offer reciprocal agreements, allowing students from neighboring states to pay in-state tuition rates.

- **Scholarships and Financial Considerations:** Most softball players often only a receive partial softball scholarship rather than a "full-ride". Most players receive a combination of both and athletic and academic scholarship. So it is important to calculate the total amount of debt you might incur throughout your college years, and consider this in your decision-making process.

4. **Communicating with College Coaches:** The best way to communicate with college coaches is by email. When you have narrowed down the colleges you want to play for, do your research. Send individual emails to each coach and assistant coach. Remember, most college coaches cannot return your emails until after September 1st of your junior year of high school, so do not get discouraged. When sending your emails, be genuine and include a link to your profile page, as well as links to any recent videos you have uploaded to the Internet. Also, include your game schedules and invite them to come watch.

    In some instances, coaches have sent their assistant coaches or even active and former players to watch you play. Always be professional, as you never know who might be watching.

SOCIAL MEDIA DOS AND DON'TS

Certainly! Creating a strong and positive online presence is essential for college softball recruiting. Here's a list of dos and don'ts to help guide potential recruits through their social media interactions.

DO:

Profile Management

- DO make sure your profiles across all social media platforms are clean and professional.

- DO use a professional-looking profile picture, ideally related to softball.

Content Sharing

- DO share your achievements, awards, and recognitions related to softball.

- DO post highlights from your games, practices, or training sessions.

- DO share content that reflects your dedication, passion, and commitment to the sport.

Engagement

- DO engage positively with coaches, teams, and other athletes. Show your support and enthusiasm.

- DO participate in relevant conversations, forums, or threads to showcase your knowledge and passion for softball.

Networking

- DO follow and engage with college coaches, softball programs, and related organizations.

- DO use social media to network with other athletes, coaches, and professionals in the softball community.

Consistency

- DO keep your social media accounts active by regularly updating them with relevant content.

DO NOT

Inappropriate Content

- DO NOT post offensive, rude, or disrespectful content. This includes comments, photos, or videos.

- DO NOT share content that you would not want a potential college coach to see.

Over-sharing

DO NOT share every aspect of your personal life. Keep your profiles focused mainly on softball and related activities.

Negative Interaction

- DO NOT engage in arguments, trolling, or negative discussions on social media.

- DO NOT speak ill of coaches, teammates, opponents, or officials.

Misrepresentation

- DO NOT exaggerate your accomplishments or skills. Be genuine and honest.

- DO NOT use someone else's content and present it as your own.

Ignoring Guidelines

- DO NOT ignore or bypass the rules and guidelines set by social media platforms.

- DO NOT ignore the NCAA's rules and regulations related to recruiting and social media interaction.

Over-Promotion

- DO NOT overly promote yourself. Be modest and let your achievements speak for themselves.

GENERAL TIPS FOR SOFTBALL PLAYERS

- Think before you post: Always consider the content and potential implications of your post before.

- **Privacy settings:** Regularly review and update your privacy settings to control who sees your content.

- **Google yourself:** Conduct regular searches of your name to see what information is publicly available.

By adhering to these guidelines, recruits can maintain a social media presence that enhances their chances of being positively noticed by college coaches and softball programs.

5. **Maintaining an Updated Player Profile:** When creating a player profile, it is advisable to save the information on a home computer instead of relying exclusively on your select team's profile page. Changing teams could result in the loss of information. Consider using third-party websites that offers the option to maintain a profile page independently of your select team page. Ensure that the profile is updated frequently to reflect any changes in your situation, adding new photos and videos as necessary.

6. **Create a YouTube Channel for Exposure:** Consider creating a YouTube channel, or similar on-line video storage platform, to display your skills videos, and

dramatic plays. This will enable you to send the links to the college coaches, keeping them up-to-date on your progress.

7. **Importance of GPA, ACT, and SAT:** The importance of your GPA, moreover, ACT and SAT scores, cannot be overstated. College coaches have a limited number of scholarships available, which they need to divide among multiple players. Scoring higher on your ACT and SAT tests can increase the amount awarded for academic scholarships. This allows college coaches to distribute their scholarship funds among a larger pool of players. Your GPA reflects your consistency and dedication as a student, and coaches use this to gauge your potential performance at the college level.

8. **Registering with the NCAA:** If you want to play softball for an NCAA college at the Division I or Division II level, it is essential to register and be cleared by the NCAA. All NCAA athletes must eventually create an account. It is recommended to create your account by the beginning of your junior year in high school to avoid the backlog of athletes attempting clearance at the end of the year.

Once your account is created, several additional steps must be completed to finalize your registration. Visit the NCAA website for registration.

9. **Upholding a Respectable Image On and Off the Field:** Your reputation follows you throughout your softball career. You do not want to be known as the player who misses practice, arrives late for games and practices, or is perceived as lazy or disrespectful towards coaches or other players. The softball community is small, and word gets around quickly. Therefore, upholding a respectable image and reputation is crucial.

10. **Wearing the Uniform with Pride:** Getting a softball scholarship is not only about showcasing your skills on the field. It is also about demonstrating seriousness and respect for the game and the college you wish to represent. Think of it like going for an important job interview; you would naturally wear your best outfit to make a good impression. When you are trying to get a softball scholarship, maintaining a neat and professional appearance from the moment you arrive at the field is important. Ensure that your uniform is clean and properly worn. Avoid undoing your pants or walking around in your sliders. Get fully dressed at home so you

arrive at the field ready to play. Maintain the neatness of your uniform, keeping it on and properly fastened even after the game ends. A uniform that ends the day dirty and sweaty is a evidence of your hard work and dedication to the game.

11. **Learning from Mistakes and Maintaining Positivity:** Softball is a game of failure. You will not always succeed; in fact, failures in the game happen more often than successes. Coaches understand this—they do not expect players to hit the ball every at bat. It is a tough game, with nine players on the opposing team trying to stop you. In the field, errors are inevitable. When they happen, figure out what went wrong and focus correcting them during practice. Do not get frustrated or upset when you make a mistake. Avoid showing negative emotions, like throwing your helmet, bat or glove in anger.

    Maintain a professional attitude, understanding that failure are part of the game. Opportunities for improvement and success will come your way. Keep your head high without showing disappointment.

12. **Creation of a Skills Video:** Skills video are the best way to demonstrate your skills and attract coaches. Your video should be brief, about 2-3 minutes, showcasing your key skills, strengths and abilities. College coaches usually prefer shorter videos. Details on how to create the video, including specifications based on player positions, will be covered in a later chapter.

13. **Avoiding Over-training in Softball:** Players often experience the detrimental effects of over-training, particularly when the drive to improve pushes them past the brink of fatigue. When frustration and exhaustion set in, the likelihood of making mistakes increases dramatically, especially in batting practice. The onset of bad habits is not just a possibility but a near certainty under these conditions. These habits, once established, become deeply ingrained and can be exceedingly stubborn, resisting efforts to correct them.

Understanding the critical moment to stop is essential for any softball player's development. It is not merely about the quantity of practice, but the quality of each movement performed. Every swing taken during practice must be done with precision. This precision is not a singular aspect but a composite of several key fundamentals: the strategic placement of the feet for stability and power, the timely rotation of the hips to generate force, the full extension of the arms to maximize reach and impact, and the discipline to keep the head down for optimal focus and eye contact with the ball.

14. **Avoid personal distractions:** Softball players should not have their cell phones out in the dugout, nor should they engage in public displays of affection with boyfriends or girlfriends during tournaments or practices. Players should not communicate with parents or fans during games. Additionally, players should refrain from non-softball-related discussions during games and remain focused on the game.

By committing to this disciplined approach, softball players can avoid the pitfalls of over-training. Each practice session should be approached with a clear intention to reinforce good habits, ensuring that every swing brings the player one step closer to batting excellence.

CHAPTER SEVEN

THE SOFTBALL COACH'S RESPONSIBILITIES

Softball coaches wear many hats: mentor, strategist, and often, life coach. A softball coach's primary duty is to encourage improvement and skill development in their players. This involves creating an environment that encourages both personal and athletic growth, ensuring that each player has the opportunity to advance in their abilities and understanding of the game. Here are some guidelines to consider.

COMPREHENSIVE TRAINING AND TEACHING SCENARIOS

Training is the foundation of any team's success, and a coach's role in this cannot be overstated. It begins with assessing the team's collective capabilities and the individual talents of each player. From there, a coach creates training plans that are both rigorous and varied, ensuring that practices simulate a wide range of in-game situations. The players then understand that true readiness comes from experiencing the unexpected during practice, so when the real challenges arise, the team can respond with confidence and agility.

PRIORITIZING ALL PLAYERS OVER WINS

A coach's commitment to each player's growth can sometimes mean making decisions that prioritize development over immediate victory. A coach should recognize that every player contributes to the team's dynamics, and that promoting everyone's talents is essential. Coaches should make it a point to give each player their moment on the field. This approach not only builds a stronger team but also instills the value of teamwork.

LEVERAGING LOSSES AS TEACHING OPPORTUNITIES

Every loss is a lesson in disguise, and a softball coach must turn these moments into opportunities for growth. Post-game, a coach should guide the team through constructive analysis, highlighting what can be learned rather than dwelling on the score. This approach encourages players to view setbacks not as failures but as steppingstones to accomplishment.

SUPPORTING STRUGGLING PLAYERS

A coach's role is never more important than when a player is facing difficulties. When a player struggles, a coach must step in with support and personalized attention. By working closely with struggling players, setting achievable goals, and celebrating small victories, a coach can help players regain confidence and improve their performance.

CREATION OF PLAYER PROFILES

Softball coaches should encourage players to create detailed profiles showcasing their skills, statistics, and personal goals. This not only helps players track their progress but also becomes a valuable tool when exploring opportunities beyond high school and select softball. By guiding players through this process, coaches ensure that their athletes are seen by college coaches.

COMMUNICATING WITH COLLEGE COACHES

The recruitment process can be intimidating for players and their families. Here, the coach acts as a conduit, helping to establish communication with college coaches. They assist players in understanding the recruitment process, preparing for showcases, and making informed decisions about their athletic and academic futures.

Important note: As a select coach, you must avoid overselling a player when communicating with college coaches. They can recognize this. It is crucial to be honest and straightforward. When a college coach needs a player with speed, point them to the fastest player on your team, even if she is not your daughter. Always suggest the player who matches the position that the college coach seeks.

In conclusion, a softball coach's responsibilities extend far beyond the tactical aspects of the game. You are there to help every player can thrive. As the team grows stronger, the values learned on the field will resonate long after the last inning is played. Through comprehensive training, prioritizing personal growth, embracing lessons from losses, supporting each player, and setting the stage for future opportunities, coaches leave an unforgettable mark on their players and the sport itself.

CHAPTER EIGHT

PARENTS' RESPONSIBILITIES

Parental involvement is essential in your player's journey, especially during the college recruitment process. Your role is not solely about attending games and cheering from the sidelines; it is about creating an environment that facilitates growth, respect, and dedication for your young player. This chapter serves as a guide to help your young player achieve their dream.

POSITIVE BEHAVIOR AT GAMES

- **Sportsmanship:** Always show respect to coaches, umpires, and opponents. Your child learns from observing your behavior.

- **Encourage, Do not Criticize:** Focus on motivating and encouraging players instead of criticizing them for mistakes during the game.

- **Avoid Confrontation:** Try to prevent arguments or confrontations with coaches, umpires, or other parents during games.

BE ON TIME FOR GAMES AND PRACTICES

- **Plan Ahead:** Make sure you and your child are aware of the schedules and plan your time accordingly to avoid rushing. Make sure your player has food, water, and other necessities.

- **Prioritize Commitments:** Understand that consistent tardiness and absences can affect team dynamics and the player's reputation. Make attending games and practices a top priority.

UNIFORM MAINTENANCE

- **Teach Responsibility:** Encourage your player to take care of their uniform. This instills discipline and shows respect for the team's image.

- **Establish Cleaning Routines:** Create a consistent schedule for laundering and maintaining uniforms and equipment. This ensures that the players' attire is always game-ready and in the best possible condition. This also applies to bats and gloves. Check batting gloves can be sweaty and begin to smell. Fielding gloves can have laces break during games and need repair, also fielding gloves need to be conditioned regularly. If you do not have glove conditioner, sunscreen works very well. Bats are especially important to keep clean. Many players rub dirt on their bats while at the plate. Tell your player to NOT do this. Having dirt on the bat is like having dirt on a road while driving, your tires will not grip the roadway, and the ball will deflect the bat upwards or downwards causing poor contact.

SUPPORT YOUR PLAYER'S PRACTICE SCHEDULE

- **Provide Practice Space:** If you have the means, allocate a specific area at home for your child to practice. This shows that you value their commitment to improvement. If home space is limited, take the initiative to locate alternate venues like local parks or sports facilities where they can train without distractions.

- Recognize the Significance of Practice: Support for the effort and time your child dedicates to practice. Recognize each practice as a steppingstone to their development and encourage them to attend team practice regularly.

PROVIDE CONSTRUCTIVE FEEDBACK

- **Encourage Open Communication:** Ensure your player feels secure enough to openly discuss their performance. This involves being an active listener, providing a safe space for them to express their athletic concerns, and sharing their ambitions. It is about creating a trusting relationship where the child knows their voice is heard and valued.

- **Maintain Objectivity:** When providing feedback, consciously separate your personal emotions from the conversation. Aim to give clear, constructive criticism that helps your player grow rather than subjective comments that could be tied to your own feelings. This objectivity helps your player to understand the feedback is a means of improvement rather than personal criticism.

- **Game Footage:** Recording game footage is one of the best ways to support your player. This footage serves two key purposes: aiding the recruiting process and enhancing training. Just as bodybuilders use mirrors to check their form, softball players benefit from seeing themselves in action, which they can't do during live play. However, it's important to introduce this tool sensitively to ensure the player does not feel criticized.

When recording game footage, focus on moments where your player demonstrates proper mechanics and fundamentals, particularly in batting. Be mindful that videos can be paused, highlighting any flawed mechanics. Here are some tips on producing quality videos:

1. **Ensure Stable Footage:** Investing in a good tripod or stabilizer can drastically improve the quality of the game footage. Stable videos allow college coaches to focus on your players' abilities without the distraction of shaky camera work.

2. Avoid Filming the Fence: Be mindful of your shooting angles so that the camera's focus remains on your player and not on obstructions like the fence. These distractions take attention away from

the player's performance. Clear footage is essential for college coaches who need to see the player's skills unobstructed.

3. **Highlight Significant Plays:** While it may be important to video the full game for context, also take the time to edit and create clips that showcase your players' best moments. This not only highlights their skills but also makes the footage more engaging for viewers, especially potential coaches.

4. **Opt for Natural Video:** Keep the video editing simple and resist the temptation to add too many special effects or dramatic edits. Recruiters are interested in evaluating true skill and play, not the video production quality. A natural, unaltered recording allows for an honest assessment of a player's abilities.

By actively taking these steps, parents reinforce not just their child's sports journey but also the foundational life skills of responsibility, dedication, and constructive self-assessment.

55

These actions demonstrate a commitment to their child's growth both on and off the field, emphasizing the value of hard work, perseverance, and resilience.

CHAPTER NINE

SOFTBALL SKILLS VIDEOS

When creating your skills video, keep in mind, college coaches have limited time and countless videos to sift through. Your skills video needs to grab attention fast, display your skills, and make a memorable impression within a 2–3-minute time-frame. Here is how:

START WITH YOUR INTRODUCTION

Stand in a well-lit area with minimal background noise. State your name, position, graduation year, and the high school team you play for. Speak clearly, confidently with a friendly voice – this is your elevator speech.

BATTING SKILLS

The first thing a coach does on game day when they step into the dugout is set their coffee down. The second thing they do is pull out a lineup card. Unless you are a pitcher only, you will need to be a hitter to be in the lineup. The importance of hitting cannot be emphasized enough. To effectively showcase your batting skills in a softball skills video, it is crucial to provide a comprehensive view of your abilities.

Here is how to set up:

- **Live Pitching or a Machine:** Begin by ensuring the footage includes you hitting either from a pitcher throwing practice fastballs or from a batting machine. This setup closely simulates a game situation and highlights your ability to handle live pitching.

- **Camera Angles for Batting:** Capture 6-10 swings from behind the batter. This angle is essential as it allows college coaches to see the ball's direction post-contact. Use caution when filming from this position as serious injury and camera damage can occur.

- **Film 6-10 swings from the batter's open side.** This perspective is important to demonstrate your stance, swing mechanics, extension, and follow-through.

BASE RUNNING, SLIDING, AND DIVING.

If you are a fast runner, make sure to showcase your speed in your skills video. Remember, you slide into bases and dive back to them.

- **Base Running from Home to First:** Set the camera on the third-base side of home plate to get a clear view. Film yourself taking a swing and running through first base. This shows your speed out of the batter's box.

- **Rounding the Bases:** Take another swing, this time demonstrate how you run the bases on a hit that allows you to go beyond first base. This part of the video should capture your speed and agility running bases.

- **Sliding Techniques:** If sliding is an important part of your game, include clips of you sliding into bases, particularly home plate. This not only shows your competitive edge but also your skill in safely evading tags.

VIDEOS BY POSITION

PITCHERS

Your video should show a comprehensive array of pitches, captured from several vantage points. Show your pitching mechanics from the side to emphasize form, capture the movement and trajectory of your pitches from behind, and demonstrate your control and pitch placement from the front. If you can, include a radar gun reading to highlight your pitch speed.

For enhanced visibility of pitches with significant movement, an indoor football facility can be an ideal location. These facilities often have clear, marked lines which can be used as a reference point. Align the pitching rubber with one of these lines, measure out the standard pitching distance of 43 feet, and place a home plate marker accordingly. Position your catcher behind home plate.

When filming from behind safety must be your top priority. The camera operator should stay vigilant as there is always a possibility of a pitch being missed by the catcher. By filming along the centerline of the field, viewers will see the ball's spin and break.

Using an indoor facility not only eliminates variables such as wind and lighting but also provides a controlled environment where your skills can truly stand out.

CATCHERS

In your softball skills video, as a catcher, you will need to demonstrate a range of abilities that are crucial for the position. Here is how to capture your capabilities effectively:

1. **Pitch Framing:** It is important to show how you handle pitches. To adequately display your pitch framing skills, record from a vantage point about 10 feet in front of the pitcher. Capture how you frame 2 to 3 pitches for each corner of the strike zone.

2. **Blocking Skills:** Your ability to block pitches is key. For optimal visibility, set the camera slightly off to one side — roughly 2 feet to the left and 5 feet in front of the pitching mound. Show how you block pitches, with 2 to 3 pitches directly ahead, to your left, and to your right.

3. Throwing Agility: Coaches are looking for quick and agile movements from catchers. To capture your pop and throwing skills, place the camera around 3 feet behind third base for 2 to 4 throws and approximately 2 feet behind the catcher for another 2 to 3 throws, showing your ability to move swiftly from a squatting position.

4. **Bunt Coverage and Throwing Accuracy:** Your ability to handle bunts and make accurate throws is crucial. Demonstrate this by filming your reaction to bunts and your subsequent throws to first base. Record these actions by placing the camera 3 feet behind the home plate for a couple of bunts and then 3 feet to the right of first base for your throws.

5. **Game Footage of Covering First Base:** If you have footage of yourself covering first base during a game, make sure to include that to provide a comprehensive view of your defensive skills. This will give coaches a complete picture of your agility and in-game decision-making.

MIDDLE INFIELDERS

Your video should show your side-to-side agility, your ability to smoothly handle routine and difficult ground balls, and the power of your throw. It is important to demonstrate dynamic and swift footwork, especially your pivoting technique and how you handle transitions when turning double plays.

For shortstops and second basemen, take all the grounders from the shortstop position to highlight your arm strength. If your primary position is second base, you can still field from there, although typically infielders showcase their throwing from shortstop.

For the video, position the camera approximately four feet to the left of the pitcher's mound for half of your throws to capture one angle. For the remainder, move the camera four feet behind first base to get a different perspective. The following should be included in your video:

- Fielding ground balls that come straight toward you

- Field 2-4 ground balls that are hit about 8-10 feet to your left

- React to 2-4 ground balls that are hit 8-10 feet to your right

- Charge 2-4 slow-rolling choppers headed straight for you

Demonstrate how you perform in double play situations by including 4-5 feeds from second base. Make sure you are crossing over the bag and executing the throw to first base.

Position the camera two feet behind the pitcher's mound for the first half of these plays and four feet behind first base for the remaining shots.

Lastly, show your fielding proficiency at the shortstop position with throws to second base. Place the camera two feet behind the pitcher's mound to video the following:

- 2 ground balls hit straight at you

- 2 ground balls hit four feet to your right

- 2 ground balls hit four feet to your left

This variety of plays will give coaches a comprehensive view of your defensive skills.

FIRST BASE

Your video should demonstrate your abilities at first base by capturing footage that highlights your ability to cover the base. Position your camera slightly to the left of home plate and behind it to ensure an optimal view. Your video should include the following and remember to finish the play. In other words, make your throws to the appropriate base.

- Field 3 to 4 ground balls straight at you

- Field 3 to 4 ground balls to your left side

- Field 3 to 4 ground balls on your right side

Additionally, include clips of yourself charging 3 to 4 bunts to show your agility.

THIRD BASE

Place the camera in front of you, about 4 feet to the right of home base, for half of your fielding drills. For the other half, set up the camera approximately 1 foot behind first base. Your softball skills video should show the following and remember to finish the play. In other words, make your throws to the appropriate base.

- Field 3-4 ground balls coming straight at you

- Field 3-4 ground balls to your left

- Field 3-4 ground balls to your right/backhand side

- Field 3-4 slow choppers aimed directly at you

- Charge 3 to 4 ground balls with a throws to 1st base

OUTFIELDERS

College coaches expect outfielders, regardless of their position, to field ground balls and fly balls from either right or center field. The reason for right field perspective is to show your arm strength from throws from right field to 3rd base. Capture this these three primary camera angles:

1. Place the camera halfway between second base (2B) and the pitcher's mound. From this angle, field two ground balls and two fly balls hit straight to you and throw them to 2B. Also, record handling grounders and fly balls hit to your left and right.

2. Install the camera directly behind third base (3B). Here, field two ground balls and two fly balls coming directly at you and throw them to 3B. Additionally, capture fielding for balls hit to both your left and right.

3. Set the camera right behind the catcher. In this setup, field two ground balls and two fly balls hit straight towards you and throw them to home plate.

Ensure the footage shows how you track and field fly balls, focusing on your arm strength and accuracy.

EDITING

Editing is crucial. Keep your video at the 2-3 minute mark. Use simple, clean transitions. Remember, the focus is on your skills, not fancy video effects.

Once edited, upload your video to a platform like YouTube or Vimeo. Set the video to public or unlisted, and you are ready to share.

Attach the link to your skill video in emails to college coaches. Be direct in your emails and encourage coaches to watch your video. Invite them to reach out with any questions or to discuss your potential contributions to their program.

Remember, this skills video is your chance to make a good first impression. Make it count, make it professional, and make it showcase the best of your abilities on the softball field.

COMMON VIDEO MISTAKES

- **Insufficient Repetitions:** The hitting segment should include 15 to 20 hits, with half of them shown from a side view (facing the camera) and the other half from behind the batter. This demonstrates where the bat makes contact and the direction of the ball on the field.

Remember to include the "plane" or path of the ball, covering high pitches, low pitches, inside pitches, and outside pitches.

- **Over Reliance on Game Footage:** While it is acceptable to use some game footage, ensure the viewer can easily identify who they are watching. Make sure you are properly labeled in the video.

- Lack of Intensity by the Player: Players should always perform at game speed during the video to accurately showcase their skills.

- Inappropriate Player Attire: Players must be properly dressed in their uniforms, avoiding casual wear such as shorts or sweatpants. Ensure that the uniform is clean. Players should have their hair styled and makeup applied for the introductory section of the video.

Important Note: Do not post videos or photographs that are unflattering or demonstrate poor mechanics, especially in relation to hitting. Ensure that your player is using proper techniques, and consult with an experienced hitting coach for guidance.

CHAPTER TEN

UNCONVENTIONAL DRILLS

RACQUETBALL COURT DRILL FOR SOFTBALL PLAYERS

I have discovered that one of the best ways to teach reaction time and fielding techniques involves the use of a racquetball court. Catching a high-speed racquetball in this court enhances reaction time and offers a great cardiovascular workout. The player can complete numerous reps in a short amount of time. Racquetballs are designed to bounce, which helps the player use both hands and secure the ball. In addition, racquetballs are softer thus reducing the fear of injury during training. While a racquetball may sting, it will not break bones. Racquetball balls are high speed and can rebound off the wall at speeds of about 120 miles per hour, making fielding a softball seem comparatively slow. Scan this QR code for a demo.

HITTING OFF AN AUTOMATED PITCHING MACHINE

When hitting off an automated pitching machine, the instructor can stand behind the hitter to evaluate each swing. When an instructor stands in front of the batter and pitches balls from behind an L screen the instructor can miss much of what the players are doing, as they are busy defending themselves. Many indoor batting facilities offer automated pitching machines, which typically throw between 15 and 20 balls per cycle.

While standing behind the batter, the instructor should focus on one aspect of the swing each day. I usually start with the feet and work upward. A strong foundation simplifies other corrections. After the player masters foot positioning and proper rotation, they will have a consistent foundation for the rest of the instruction. It is important not to overwhelm the player with too many instructions at once. Focus on one area until the player shows consistency, then proceed to the next.

During these drills, it is important to let the player know that swinging and missing the ball is okay. If a player becomes frustrated, calm them down and reassure them that this is part of fixing the swing.

Avoid over training. When players get tired, they begin to develop bad habits. Generally, it only takes 12 improper swings to form a bad habit, so be vigilant.

THE BAT THROW DRILL

The bat throw drill is one of the easiest methods for teaching and correcting hitting mechanics. 80% of the hitting fundamentals can be achieved with this simple drill.

Instruct your player to stand at the plate on an empty field and throw the bat toward center field. Ensure the field is clear of others for safety and use old bats to avoid damaging good

bats. For right-handed batters, bats going to the right field indicate an early release, while bats to the left field signify a late release; the opposite applies for left-handed batters.

After throwing the bat, the player should retrieve it and repeat the process, ideally about 20 times per session to avoid excessive fatigue.

This drill teaches the player to load her weight onto her back leg, stride with the front foot, rotate the hips, pull with the front elbow, push with the back elbow, and extend the bat through the hitting zone. It also ensures the bat plane is maintained at the proper angle. This drill is perfect for beginners and is equally beneficial for more advanced hitters to reinforce fundamental techniques.

CHAPTER ELEVEN

SOFTBALL PLAYER'S COLLEGE RECRUITING CHECKLIST

Commit to Training

- Establish a consistent training schedule.

- Identify areas of strength and areas that need improvement.

- Find a mentor or coach for guidance.

- Track progress regularly.

Set Career Goals and Select a Major

- Set short-term and long-term career goals.

- Research possible majors that align with career goals.

- Seek advice from school counselors or mentors.

Research Potential Colleges

- Create a list of colleges based on academic and athletic preferences.

- Visit campus facilities and talk to students/athletes.

- Evaluate scholarship opportunities.

Network with College Coaches

- Identify coaches from colleges of interest.

- Initiate communication through emails.

- Attend softball camps or recruitment events.

Social Media Dos and Don'ts

- Post content that aligns with personal and professional goals.

- Avoid sharing inappropriate or divisive content.

- Post on all platforms

- Follow the coaches, assistant coaches, and teams you wish to play for.

Maintain an Updated Player Profile

- Update stats and achievements regularly.

- Collect references or endorsements.

- Share profile with coaches and assistant coaches.

Create a YouTube Channel for Exposure

- Establish a channel dedicated to showcasing skills.

- Regularly upload videos from games or training sessions.

- Share the channel link with the coaches you want to play for.

Academics: The Importance of GPA, ACT, and SAT

- Maintain a high GPA throughout high school.

- Prepare for and take the ACT/SAT exams.

- Participate in academic workshops or tutoring if needed.

Register with the NCAA

- Understand NCAA eligibility requirements.

- Complete the NCAA registration process.

- Stay updated with any changes to NCAA regulations.

Uphold a Respectable Image On and Off the Field

- Behave professionally during games and events.

- Avoid engaging in activities that might tarnish reputation.

- Develop positive relationships with teammates, coaches, and the community.

Wear your Uniform with Pride

- Ensure the uniform is clean and in good condition.

- Wear the uniform correctly, adhering to team guidelines.

- Remember that when wearing the uniform, you not only represent yourself but also the team and other teammates.

Learn from Mistakes and Maintaining a Positive Attitude

- Reflect on feedback from coaches and peers.

- Use mistakes as learning opportunities.

- Stay motivated and focus on self-improvement.

Create a Skills Video

- Emphasize your key skills.

- Film high-quality footage during games or practice.

- Edit the video for clarity and impact and upload it to YouTube and share directly with coaches.

Notes

Notes

Notes

Notes

ABOUT THE AUTHOR

Howard E. Deihl, RHU

Since I stepped onto the softball field in 1992 as a fastpitch softball coach, I have dedicated most of my free time to mastering and teaching the art of fastpitch softball. As the former owner and founder of Homerun Alley, a training facility I owned and operated for eight years, I transformed it into a hub of fastpitch softball excellence. It was staffed with a team of coaches, predominantly former Division 1 softball players. This environment not only refined players' skills but also prepared them for competitive play at various levels.

My expertise in batting instruction stands out among my accomplishments. I have developed and implemented unique training programs that rapidly enhance players' hitting and fielding abilities. These programs have proven effective time and again, helping players to improve their game significantly.

Coaching fastpitch softball has taken me across the country, leading a coast-to-coast travel team and exposing players to diverse competitive teams. This experience has enriched my coaching approach, allowing me to adapt to various playing styles and conditions.

I take particular pride in my role guiding players to secure softball scholarships across all divisions, from NCAA to NAIA, and from Division 1 to junior college. My extensive experience in the recruiting process has been a key factor in helping players achieve their dreams of playing softball at higher levels.

In essence, my career in fastpitch softball is more than just coaching; it's about inspiring and guiding players, improving their skills, and opening doors to new opportunities in the sport.

Once again, special thanks to
Taylor Weatherford
for making the book cover so appealing!

www.ingramcontent.com/pod-product-compliance
Lightning Source LLC
Chambersburg PA
CBHW071549150726
48000CB00002B/988